MYSTERIOUS MUMMIES

by Fiona Macdonald

Gareth Stevens Publishing
A WORLD ALMANAC EDUCATION GROUP COMPANY

Please visit our web site at: **www.garethstevens.com**
For a free color catalog describing Gareth Stevens Publishing's
list of high-quality books and multimedia programs,
call 1-800-542-2595 (USA) or 1-800-387-3178 (Canada).
Gareth Stevens Publishing's fax: (414) 332-3567.

Library of Congress Cataloging-in-Publication Data

Macdonald, Fiona.
   Mysterious mummies / by Fiona Macdonald. — North American ed.
     p. cm. — (History hunters)
   Includes bibliographical references and index.
   ISBN 0-8368-3742-8 (lib. bdg.)
   1. Mummies—Egypt—Juvenile literature. 2. Egypt—Antiquities—Juvenile literature.
   3. Excavations (Archaeology)—Egypt—Juvenile literature. I. Title. II. Series.
  DT62.M7M94   2003
  932—dc21   2003045666

This North American edition first published in 2004 by
Gareth Stevens Publishing
A World Almanac Education Group Company
330 West Olive Street, Suite 100
Milwaukee, WI 53212 USA

This U.S. edition copyright © 2004 by Gareth Stevens, Inc. Original edition copyright © 2003 ticktock
Entertainment Ltd. First published in Great Britain in 2003 by ticktock Media Ltd., Unit 2, Orchard Business
Centre, North Farm Road, Tunbridge Wells, Kent, TN2 3XF. Additional end matter copyright © 2004 by
Gareth Stevens, Inc.

We would like to thank: David Gillingwater, Dr. Richard Parkinson at The British Museum,
and Elizabeth Wiggans.

Gareth Stevens editor: Carol Ryback
Gareth Stevens cover design: Katherine A. Goedheer

Photo credits:
t=top, b=bottom, c=center, l=left, r=right, OFC=outside front cover, OBC=outside back cover

Alamy images: OFCl, 3b, 4tr, 5tl, 10tr, 11b, 12tr, 14tr, 14br, 16br, 20cb, 24br, 26tr, 26b. Corbis:
OFCbr, 4tc, 6tr, 6-7c, 7tl, 8tr, 8bc, 8-9b, 9cr, 10-11c, 11tr, 12cr, 12-13, 15tr, 16-17c, 19cr, 23c,
26-27c, 28-29c, 29cl. Heritage Images: 9t. Popperfoto: 22tr. Science Photo Library: 22cr, 24tr,
25tl, 25tr.

Printed in Hong Kong

1 2 3 4 5 6 7 8 9 07 06 05 04 03

Would you like to join an exciting expedition to Egypt?

The characters accompanying you — Will Yates, Dr. Jane Smith, and Dr. Mokhtar Ahmad — are fictitious, but the facts about Egyptologists, archaeologists, and scientists represent an accurate view of their work. The tomb you are about to discover and the mummy buried inside are also fictitious, but the characteristics of the mummy and details from the excavation are based on actual discoveries made in Egypt.

Can't wait to learn more? Ready to dig for ancient clues?

Then welcome to the City Museum...

CONTENTS

TREASURES IN THE ATTIC 4
A TRIP TO EGYPT 6
EARLY EGYPTIAN EXPLORERS 8
A DAY IN CAIRO 10
AT THE PYRAMIDS 12
THE NILE RIVER 14
AT THE DIG SITE 16
A TOMB IN THE DESERT 18
TREASURES IN THE SAND 20
INSIDE THE TOMB 22
THE MUMMY'S SECRETS 24
PRESERVING THE MUMMY 26
THE PRINCESS MUMMY 28
GLOSSARY 30
MORE INFORMATION/INDEX 32

CITY MUSEUM PASS

Name: Dr. Jane Smith
Position: Curator
Department: Ancient Egyptian Antiquities

Interests: Ancient civilizations, travel, and digging in ruins.

CITY MUSEUM PASS

Name: Will Yates
Position: Research Assistant
Department: Ancient Egyptian Antiquities

Interests: Ancient history, computers, and old horror movies.

TEMPORARY

Day 1

Wow! Today has been very exciting. We visited Dr. Smith, a curator at the City Museum, to show her what we found in the attic. There's an old, yellowed diary and some postcards, a tiny statue, a golden beetle, and some tools. Dad thinks that my great-grandpa brought all that stuff home from Egypt.

Dr. Smith showed me around behind the scenes at the museum. I saw computers, a library packed with all kinds of books, storage shelves piled high with labeled boxes, and a huge, modern laboratory. The laboratory is where they "conserve" (maintain and keep safe) materials in their collections.

Dr. Smith is an Egyptologist, an expert on ancient Egypt. She looked over the items we brought in. She thinks that Great-Grandpa may have found an important site — maybe even an ancient Egyptian tomb!

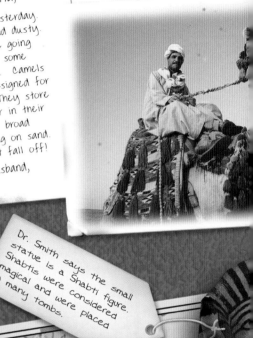

November 1, 1935
Mrs. Henrietta Yates

My dear Henrietta,

Arrived safely yesterday. It is very hot and dusty. Tomorrow, we are going by camel to see some interesting ruins. Camels are perfectly designed for desert travel. They store gallons of water in their bodies and have broad feet for walking on sand. I hope I don't fall off!

Your loving husband,
Bertie

Dr. Smith says the small statue is a Shabti figure. Shabtis were considered magical and were placed in many tombs.

France
Italy
Spain
Greece
Turkey
Mediterranean Sea
Tunisia
Morocco
Libya
Egypt
Saudi Arabia
Algeria
Western Sahara
Red Sea
Mauritania
Mali
Niger
Chad
Sudan
Eritrea
Nigeria
Ethiopia
Central African Republic
Cameroon
Democratic Republic of the Congo
Kenya

Great-Grandpa explored Egypt. It's in the northeastern corner of Africa.

Dr. Smith says that winter is the digging season in Egypt because temperatures are cooler.

Ancient Egyptians used this golden beetle — called a "scarab" — as a good-luck charm.

November 18, 1935

Another hard day spent digging. Found some strange artifacts and a huge piece of stone covered with carvings. Am not yet sure what they are or why they are here. Leaving for home next week, but I will sketch the area where I made the discoveries, and I will try to find the site when I return next year.

my old friend Ibrahim helped me explore my first ancient Egyptian site.

From: Dr. Jane Smith, The City Museum
To: Dr. Mokhtar Ahmad, Cairo, Egypt
Subject: An interesting new discovery!

Dear Mokhtar,
Someone brought in a collection of ancient Egyptian objects and an interesting old diary. I think these items could be clues to an important site. The diary contains only a rough sketch of the area as well as a faded, scribbled name — Munkfai — of the location. How will we ever find it again? Please, can you help us?

From: Dr. Mokhtar Ahmad, Cairo, Egypt
To: Dr. Jane Smith, The City Museum

Dear Jane,
I'm afraid we cannot find Munkfai on our maps. Perhaps the person who wrote the diary did not understand Arabic, our language, and mislabeled it. We could explore the region while comparing the old sketch with the landscape to locate the area.

A TRIP TO EGYPT

Day 21

We are on a plane flying over Egypt! I'm so excited. I couldn't believe it when Dr. Smith told me that her old friend, Dr. Ahmad, was planning an expedition to learn more about the place Great-Grandpa found. I was even more surprised when she said I could come along as her research assistant.

Our plane will land soon. From my window, I can see the famous pyramids, the desert, and the Nile River. At first we'll stay in Cairo — that's Egypt's modern capital city. It's strange to think that it didn't exist in ancient Egyptian times. The Nile flows right through Cairo. Buildings line both banks of the river. In ancient Egyptian times, cities were only built on the eastern bank. I've sketched out a map of Egypt showing the most important ancient and modern sites.

The airplane meal included mezze. This is a delicious traditional Egyptian snack that includes bread, hummus, olives, and stuffed grape leaves.

The Nile River flows through the bustling, modern city of Cairo.

The Sahara is the world's largest desert. It stretches across northern Africa and dominates the landscape of many African countries, including Egypt.

Map of Egypt along the banks of the Nile River.

Mediterranean Sea

Great Pyramids Giza

Lower Egypt

Cairo

Saqqara – a huge, ancient cemetery

N
W E
S

Memphis – ancient capital of Lower Egypt

Lake Karun

Fertile land

Upper Egypt

Nile River flows north

West bank of the Nile – "The land of the dead."

East bank of the Nile – "The land of the living."

Red Sea

Valley of the Kings

Thebes – ancient capital of Upper Egypt – and Karnak – a massive temple complex

Desert oasis

Desert

Abu Simbel – temples and huge statues

Aswan High Dam – controls flooding of the Nile.

From: Dr. Mokhtar Ahmad, Cairo, Egypt
To: Dr. Jane Smith, The City Museum
Subject: Good news! Come quickly!

Dear Jane,

We think we've found the site mentioned in the old diary! It's in a remote part of Egypt on the west bank of the Nile. The ancient Egyptians associated dying with the setting of the Sun. The Sun sets in the west, so they buried their dead on the Nile's west bank. We found the site completely by chance. One of my colleagues recognized the land formation from a picture in a newspaper article about a new hotel that is planned for the area. We contacted the developers, and they are going to start work soon. We plan to explore the site as quickly as possible. Care to join us? It would be wonderful to see you again.

Carter carries items from the tomb. He was the first person in more than 3,250 years to look inside Tutankhamun's tomb.

Tutankhamun's Tomb

Day 22

I've just spent a fascinating afternoon with Dr. Ahmad, learning as much as possible about Egypt and ancient Egyptian tombs. I also wanted to learn more about archaeologists — the scientists who study past human life by excavating and investigating everyday items. Dr. Ahmad showed me an old illustration and some battered black-and-white photographs of early archaeologists at work in Egypt. Then he showed me the layout of one of the most famous tombs ever discovered — Tutankhamun's (King Tut's) tomb.

Tutankhamun became pharaoh (that was what the ancient Egyptians called their kings) when he was just nine years old, in 1336 B.C. When he died at age 18, he was buried in an underground tomb on the west bank of the Nile in a place called the Valley of the Kings. Archaeologist Howard Carter discovered King Tut's tomb in 1922. Dr. Smith says that no other single excavation has given us so much evidence about life in ancient Egypt.

The burial chamber

This room contained three coffins — one inside the other. The last one, made of solid gold, held Tutankhamun's mummified (preserved) body.

THE DISCOVERY

When Carter and his team excavated Tutankhamun's tomb, they found it contained four rooms. It took ten years to carefully empty the tomb of all its treasures.

The annex

(extra storage space)

the antechamber

1923 — Howard Carter inspects the site.

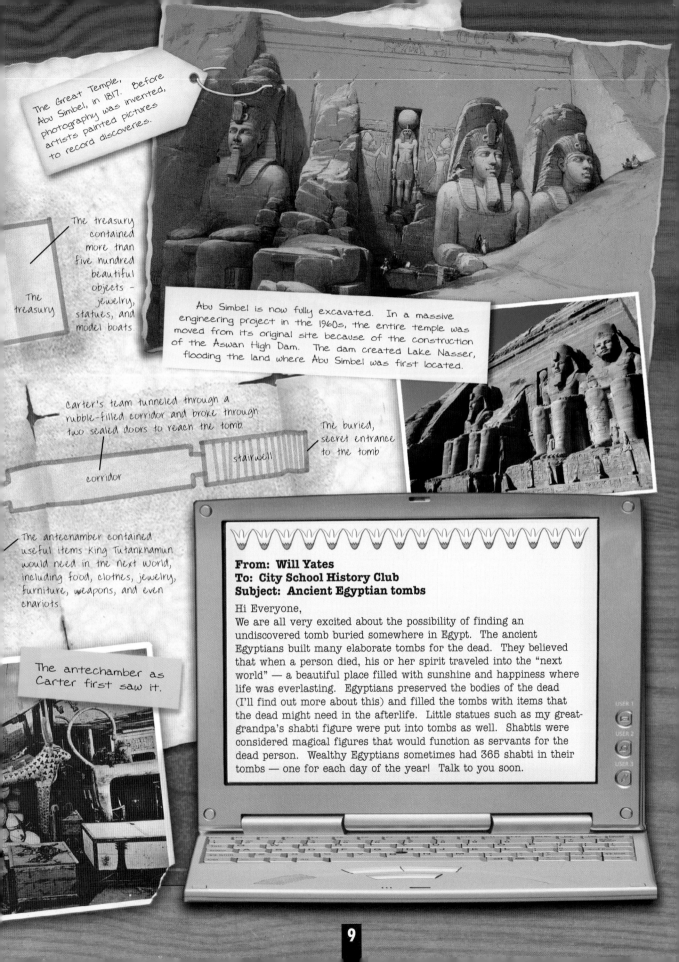

The Great Temple, Abu Simbel, in 1817. Before photography was invented, artists painted pictures to record discoveries.

The treasury contained more than five hundred beautiful objects — jewelry, statues, and model boats.

The treasury

Abu Simbel is now fully excavated. In a massive engineering project in the 1960s, the entire temple was moved from its original site because of the construction of the Aswan High Dam. The dam created Lake Nasser, flooding the land where Abu Simbel was first located.

Carter's team tunneled through a rubble-filled corridor and broke through two sealed doors to reach the tomb.

The buried, secret entrance to the tomb

stairwell

corridor

The antechamber contained useful items King Tutankhamun would need in the next world, including food, clothes, jewelry, furniture, weapons, and even chariots.

The antechamber as Carter first saw it.

From: Will Yates
To: City School History Club
Subject: Ancient Egyptian tombs

Hi Everyone,
We are all very excited about the possibility of finding an undiscovered tomb buried somewhere in Egypt. The ancient Egyptians built many elaborate tombs for the dead. They believed that when a person died, his or her spirit traveled into the "next world" — a beautiful place filled with sunshine and happiness where life was everlasting. Egyptians preserved the bodies of the dead (I'll find out more about this) and filled the tombs with items that the dead might need in the afterlife. Little statues such as my great-grandpa's shabti figure were put into tombs as well. Shabtis were considered magical figures that would function as servants for the dead person. Wealthy Egyptians sometimes had 365 shabti in their tombs — one for each day of the year! Talk to you soon.

USER 1
USER 2
USER 3

A DAY IN CAIRO

Day 23

This morning we headed straight for Cairo's Egyptian Museum. During the nineteenth century, treasure hunters flocked to Egypt. They collected ancient objects and sold them for as much money as possible. Items that didn't sell were simply thrown away.

In 1835, the Egyptian government set up a museum to collect, preserve, and store treasures from archaeological sites. Our first stop was the gallery containing more than 1,700 items found in Tutankhamun's tomb.

I couldn't wait to see Tutankhamun's famous gold death mask. This magnificent mask is made from two layers of gold hammered together and inlaid with semiprecious stones. It weighs just over 22 pounds (10 kg) and is about 21 inches (54 cm) high.

I also wanted to learn more about shabtis, the little statues found in many tombs. Shabtis could be carved from wood or stone, molded from clay or glass, cast from bronze or wax, or shaped by hand from faience — a type of glazed ceramic material.

Tutankhamun's Death Mask
The gold death mask shows a portrait of Tutankhamun. Death masks were placed over the faces of mummies to help spirits recognize the dead.

Ancient Egyptian Crafts — Making a Shabti

Step 1 Make the faience by adding lime and ash to crushed quartz. Mix with water to make a paste.

Step 2 Shape it by hand to look like a mummy.

Step 3 Let it dry.

Step 4 Rub the surface with a pebble for a smooth, shiny finish. (This is called burnishing.)

Step 5 Paint on extra details, if required.

Step 6 Place the figure on a metal grid at the bottom of a brick kiln.

Step 7 Light a fire underneath to bake, or "fire," the clay.

Tomb Paintings (Murals)
Painted scenes showing the dead person's journey to the "next world" decorated the tombs. The Egyptians believed that the dead faced many tests. In one test, spirits in the next world would weigh the dead person's heart. If the heart was heavier than expected, it meant the dead person had led a bad life. Ammut — a mythical, crocodile-headed creature — would then eat the heart. Because the Egyptians believed the dead person's soul lived in the heart, that person could never reach the next world.

This wall mural shows Tutankhamun being welcomed into the realm of the dead by the ancient Egyptian goddess, Nut.

Anubis
The ancient Egyptians had many gods. This is a statue of Anubis, the jackal-headed god of the dead.

Fit for a King
This magnificent coffin is made of gold-covered wood studded with pieces of crimson glass and blue pottery. It is the second (middle) of the three glittering coffins that held the mummified remains of King Tutankhamun.

THE NILE RIVER

Day 25

We are on our way to Great-Grandpa's site, traveling south from Cairo in a sports-utility vehicle. A camel would have been more traditional. We're heading for the desert, but so far we've stayed close to the Nile River. Most people live along the river, just like in ancient Egyptian times. For centuries, from June to September, the Nile flooded the land on either side of its banks. But since the 1960s, the floods have been controlled by the massive Aswan High Dam. Outside of a few desert oases (water holes where plants and trees grow) the Nile is the only source of water in Egypt. For the ancient Egyptians, the Nile was like a highway – sailing down the river was by far the quickest way to travel!

Dr. Smith says the climate hasn't changed much over the centuries. It hardly ever rains and is very hot in the daytime, but it is very cold at night.

Before the Aswan High Dam was built in the 1960s, the pyramid complex at Giza was affected by the Nile's annual flooding.

The Nile is the longest river in the world. It flows north for 4,160 miles (6,695 kilometers) from Lake Victoria in East Africa to the Mediterranean Sea.

Ancient Egypt had few trees. Most boats were built from bundles of papyrus, a tough reed that grows on the banks of the Nile.

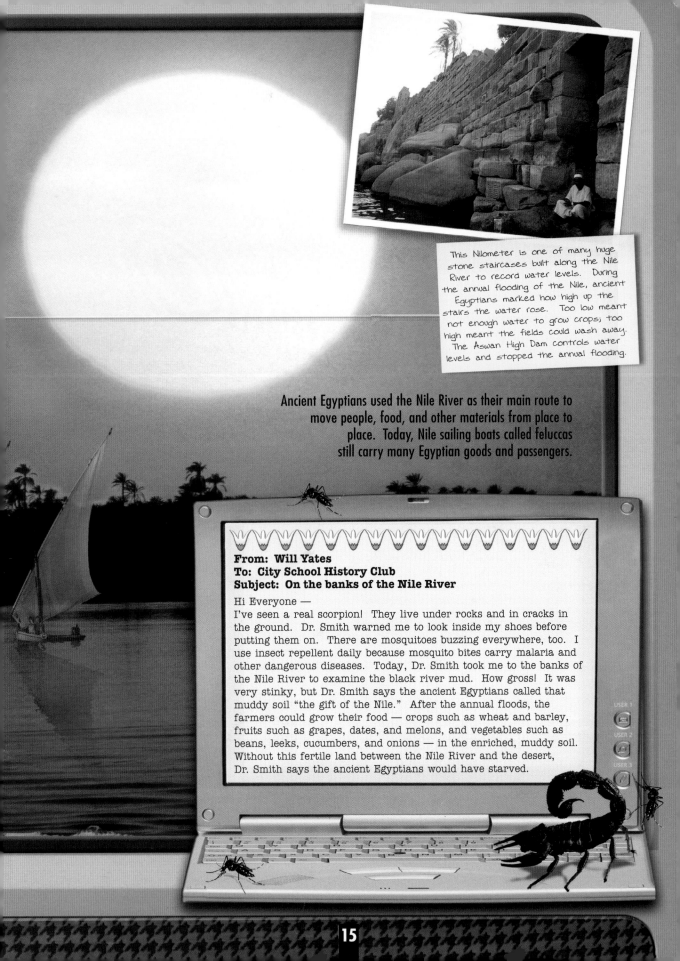

This Nilometer is one of many huge stone staircases built along the Nile River to record water levels. During the annual flooding of the Nile, ancient Egyptians marked how high up the stairs the water rose. Too low meant not enough water to grow crops; too high meant the fields could wash away. The Aswan High Dam controls water levels and stopped the annual flooding.

Ancient Egyptians used the Nile River as their main route to move people, food, and other materials from place to place. Today, Nile sailing boats called feluccas still carry many Egyptian goods and passengers.

From: Will Yates
To: City School History Club
Subject: On the banks of the Nile River

Hi Everyone —
I've seen a real scorpion! They live under rocks and in cracks in the ground. Dr. Smith warned me to look inside my shoes before putting them on. There are mosquitoes buzzing everywhere, too. I use insect repellent daily because mosquito bites carry malaria and other dangerous diseases. Today, Dr. Smith took me to the banks of the Nile River to examine the black river mud. How gross! It was very stinky, but Dr. Smith says the ancient Egyptians called that muddy soil "the gift of the Nile." After the annual floods, the farmers could grow their food — crops such as wheat and barley, fruits such as grapes, dates, and melons, and vegetables such as beans, leeks, cucumbers, and onions — in the enriched, muddy soil. Without this fertile land between the Nile River and the desert, Dr. Smith says the ancient Egyptians would have starved.

Day 26

I'm exhausted from driving across the desert. There are no roads, and the ground is very bumpy. We finally arrived and found the site by comparing the sketch in Great-Grandpa's diary with some rocks we saw on the horizon. As we got closer, we could also see the archaeologists and teams of laborers already working on the site.

The workers dug a trench across one side of the site. Then they mapped out the area using pegs with string stretched across to make a large grid. The lead archaeologist drew a map to correspond with the grid. The points on the grid are used to record the position of all objects uncovered on the site. We must mark where everything is before moving it. We could hardly wait to discover what the workers had found. "Nothing yet," they said. "Maybe this isn't the right place after all." Oh, no!

Archaeologists slowly and carefully use soft brushes and trowels to remove layers of soil from the site.

We used Great-Grandpa's sketch to find the site.

GRID SHEET

Z A →
↓
Y
Key to map of site

1. Outcrop of rocky hills
X
2. Large rocks

3. Main trench
W
4. Palm tree stumps

5. Mud bricks
V
6. A Roman coin

7. Stony areas
U

Archaeologists wear masks to avoid breathing in dust. Helmets protect their heads from falling stones and collapsing trenches.

Artifacts are labeled with the coordinates of where on the site they were found.

Striped poles and long tape measures marked in meters and centimeters are used to measure the site and record the position of artifacts.

Sand and soil are gently shaken through a fine metal screen to collect tiny fragments, such as teeth or seeds.

A TOMB IN THE DESERT

Day 30

Yesterday was terrible. We found absolutely nothing. At lunchtime, some huge earth-moving equipment arrived and parked near our site. Soon, a surveyor and an engineer came over to us. They said work was about to begin on a new hotel at the site.

We dug for the rest of the day but found nothing. Then first thing this morning, something amazing happened. The earth-mover's back wheels sank into the sand and gravel. As the driver tried to clear the sand from the wheels, he discovered a chunk of rock covered in elaborate carvings.

Dr. Smith immediately recognized the carvings as hieroglyphics – the picture writing used by the ancient Egyptians. Dr. Smith explained that there are about 1,000 different picture symbols. Each symbol represents a sound, a person, an object, or an idea. Temples and tombs were covered in hieroglyphics. Now we think we discovered the entrance to an ancient underground tomb!

The ground collapsed under the weight of the heavy machinery.

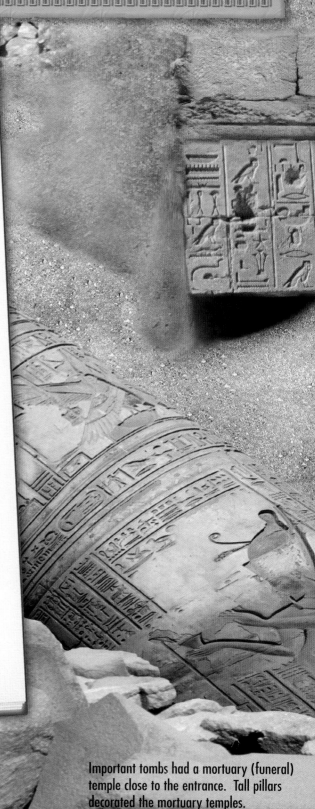

Important tombs had a mortuary (funeral) temple close to the entrance. Tall pillars decorated the mortuary temples.

Pottery containing bread, meat (usually roasted duck), beer, water, or wine were left in tombs as offerings to feed the spirit of the dead person.

Stele — slabs of wood or stone decorated with paintings or carvings — marked important tombs. Hieroglyphics often included the name of the dead person.

The Rosetta stone at the British Museum in London.

From: Dr. Mokhtar Ahmad, Cairo, Egypt
To: Will Yates
Subject: Ancient Egyptian Hieroglyphics

Dear Will,

The carvings you describe are hieroglyphics. They were invented about 3100 B.C., mostly for writing religious or royal texts. Very few ancient Egyptians could read or write. Those who could were called scribes. Scribes held the most important jobs, like working in the temples or keeping records for the pharaoh. Early archaeologists couldn't read the carvings, but in 1822, French scholar Jean-Francois Champollion cracked the hieroglyphic code using the Rosetta stone. The Rosetta stone was carved with the same message in three different languages — hieroglyphics, demotic writing (a cursive-style, simplified form of hieroglyphics used by Egyptian priests), and ancient Greek. Champollion used his knowledge of ancient Greek to crack the code of — or decipher — the other two!

USER 1
USER 2
USER 3

TREASURES IN THE SAND

Day 35

I'm hot, exhausted, and I ache all over. The developers have agreed to postpone their work, but we still have no time to waste. Dr. Smith said I can help with the dig, but I must be very careful because inexperienced diggers can accidentally damage artifacts. I've spent the last few days on my hands and knees gently sweeping away layers of sand with a brush. Our hard work has paid off. We've uncovered an underground passageway and some awesome Egyptian treasures!

Ancient tomb robbers beat us to this site. We found some of the equipment they used to break into the tomb – stone hammers with wooden handles, saws and chisels with copper blades, and reed baskets for carrying their loot. Luckily, they dropped lots of items, for we've found many artifacts buried in the sand outside the tomb, including a pair of gold earrings. Only the rich could afford gold jewelry, so Dr. Smith thinks the tomb was built for a rich person – maybe even a pharaoh or a princess!

DESIGNERS IN THE DESERT

Many paintings and statues give clues about the fashion sense of ancient Egyptians. Wealthy women wore long dresses of fine white linen, crinkled into hundreds of clinging pleats. See-through tunics of netting were decorated with glass beads and accented with wide, jeweled collars. Sandals made from plaited papyrus reeds completed the best-dressed look.

Glass was made from sand and natron (a salty chemical). This glass bottle was probably used for skin-softening, scented oils.

This dish has a handle shaped like a slave girl. It contained traces of a colored powder – probably some type of cosmetic.

These fragments of smashed faience could be the remains of shabti dropped by the tomb robbers as they ran away.

A damaged section from a jeweled collar contains pieces of blue lapis lazuli. These collars were worn over dresses and tunics.

From: Will Yates
To: Kate Yates, City College
Subject: Ancient Egyptian beauty tips

Hi Sis,

The dig is going very well. You are going to love what we found today — some 3,500-year-old makeup. Dr. Smith warned me not to touch it because it might be full of ancient germs. Apparently, both men and women wore makeup in ancient Egypt. They used crushed black or green stone mixed with water for eyeliner and powdered red ocher (an ore pigment) mixed with animal fat to color their cheeks and lips. They also wore perfume. I know that because we've found an actual perfume bottle. And although I knew ancient Egyptian women liked to wear long, curly, or plaited (braided) wigs made from human hair — I didn't know they shaved their heads underneath!

USER 1
USER 2
USER 3

Egyptologists use tweezers to pick up very delicate or tiny objects.

INSIDE THE TOMB

Day 42

Now I know how Howard Carter felt. The passage into the tomb was almost blocked where the roof had collapsed. It was too dangerous for a person to squeeze through, so the team decided to use an experimental, remote-controlled robot. The robot's camera sent back pictures to a special computer monitor. At first, the screen was blank. Then flickering images of wall murals and carvings appeared. The robot moved slowly, but when it turned its lights toward the center of the burial chamber, we found ourselves face-to-face with a beautiful mummy!

Dr. Smith explained that the ancient Egyptians preserved their bodies in order to fully enjoy the "next world." Egypt's hot, dry atmosphere naturally dries out corpses — but the mummification process developed by the ancient Egyptians kept dead bodies preserved for centuries.

Archaeology Today — Special Report
Robot Archaeologist

Testing a robot designed to explore a small shaft inside the Great Pyramid.

An extraordinary engineering feat — this compact robot navigates narrow places and collects a huge amount of scientific data. Technology like this remote-controlled robot allows archaeologists to investigate small or dangerous spaces using fiber-optic cameras.

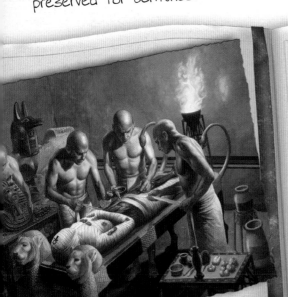

How to make a mummy

Remove the brain with a metal hook through the nose. Cut open the body's left side and remove the internal organs. Store the organs in stone vessels called canopic jars. Rinse the empty body with wine and spices, and pack it full of natron. Cover the body with natron, and leave for up to 70 days. The natron will absorb water from the flesh. Place the heart back in the body, and wrap the dried body in linen bandages soaked in resin (sap from plants). Give the finished mummy and the canopic jars to the dead person's relatives. They will place the body in a decorated coffin for burial in a tomb. (Recorded by Herodotus, the Greek traveler and scholar who visited Egypt about 500 B.C.)

Image 1

← 16.00 hours
At last we've reached the entrance to the burial chamber. It's guarded by a false door with carvings. The door allowed the mummy's spirit to travel between the worlds of the living and the dead.

17.30 hours →
Shabtis shimmer in the darkness. They look just like the one Great-Grandpa brought back from Egypt!

Image 2

6.2
6.5
6.4
6.5
7.0

Image 3

18.00 hours
She's beautiful! The serene face of an Egyptian princess smiles at us from her 3,500-year-old tomb. Her mummified body lies safely inside. The magnificent coffin is made of linen and papyrus mixed with plaster and decorated with gold. The coffin shows her wearing eye makeup, a glamorous wig, and a wide, jeweled collar. Looks like the princess wanted to look her best for the "next world."

THE MUMMY'S SECRETS

Six months later

It's great to be back in Egypt, if only for a few days. The Egyptian archaeologists were given extra time to excavate the tomb properly, and now Dr. Smith is taking me to visit the experts who have been investigating "our" mummy.

Dr. Smith laughed when I asked how they would unwrap her. She said I was very old-fashioned. Archaeologists today try not to cut open or unwrap mummies. Instead, they use X rays, CT scans, and endoscopes to "see" inside the bandages without disturbing them. X rays of bones tell archaeologists whether mummies were male or female, approximately how old they were when they died, and even whether or not they were well fed. I can't wait to see inside that beautiful gold coffin.

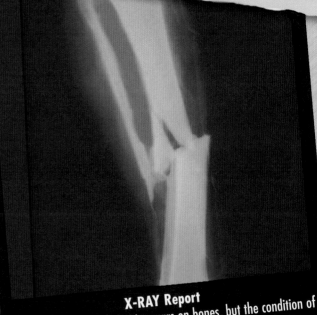

CT — computed tomography — scanners take cross-sectional images, or profiles, at 5-mm intervals (separations). A computer rearranges the profiles to create a two-dimensional picture of the inside of the mummy on a monitor. The images can be viewed from any angle for a virtual 3-D effect.

November 25, 1935

Visited my old college friend, Brown, who is digging near Cairo. Found him busily unwrapping a mummy to get at the bones inside. He was surrounded by tangled pieces of bandage. It's a shame to destroy something so old, but it's the only way to increase our knowledge of ancient life.

X-RAY Report

Malnutrition leaves distinctive scars on bones, but the condition of our mummy's bones suggests she was well nourished. The X ray also revealed an injury. This broken leg might have resulted from a fall, but the leg could have been snapped by a crocodile! Many Egyptians were attacked by crocodiles as they bathed in the Nile River. They suffered horrible bites and broken bones, lost arms and legs, or were sometimes killed.

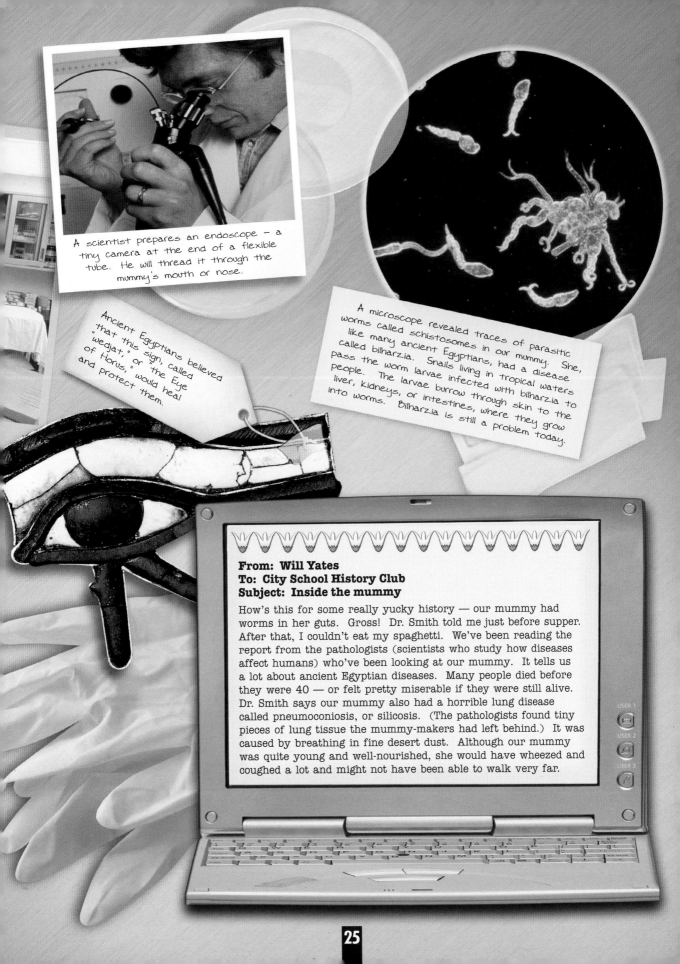

A scientist prepares an endoscope — a tiny camera at the end of a flexible tube. He will thread it through the mummy's mouth or nose.

Ancient Egyptians believed that this sign, called "wedjat," or the Eye of Horus," would heal and protect them.

A microscope revealed traces of parasitic worms called schistosomes in our mummy. She, like many ancient Egyptians, had a disease called bilharzia. Snails living in tropical waters pass the worm larvae infected with bilharzia to people. The larvae burrow through skin to the liver, kidneys, or intestines, where they grow into worms. Bilharzia is still a problem today.

From: Will Yates
To: City School History Club
Subject: Inside the mummy

How's this for some really yucky history — our mummy had worms in her guts. Gross! Dr. Smith told me just before supper. After that, I couldn't eat my spaghetti. We've been reading the report from the pathologists (scientists who study how diseases affect humans) who've been looking at our mummy. It tells us a lot about ancient Egyptian diseases. Many people died before they were 40 — or felt pretty miserable if they were still alive. Dr. Smith says our mummy also had a horrible lung disease called pneumoconiosis, or silicosis. (The pathologists found tiny pieces of lung tissue the mummy-makers had left behind.) It was caused by breathing in fine desert dust. Although our mummy was quite young and well-nourished, she would have wheezed and coughed a lot and might not have been able to walk very far.

In the laboratory

I've seen our mummy! We went to the laboratory, here in Egypt, where she's being cleaned, checked, and treated with chemicals. She will be stored at the correct temperature and humidity to help prevent further decay. Dr. Smith says this is called "conservation."

The mummy was much smaller than I expected. I was surprised to see how shriveled and leathery she looked where the bandages had slipped away from her skin. Dr. Smith explained that a human body is about 75 percent water. The natron dries up all the water during the mummification process, so the mummy shrinks as it dries.

The conservators showed us the other objects from the tomb, too. They also let us see the latest X rays. Guess what? The X rays show she was stabbed. Our mummy was murdered!

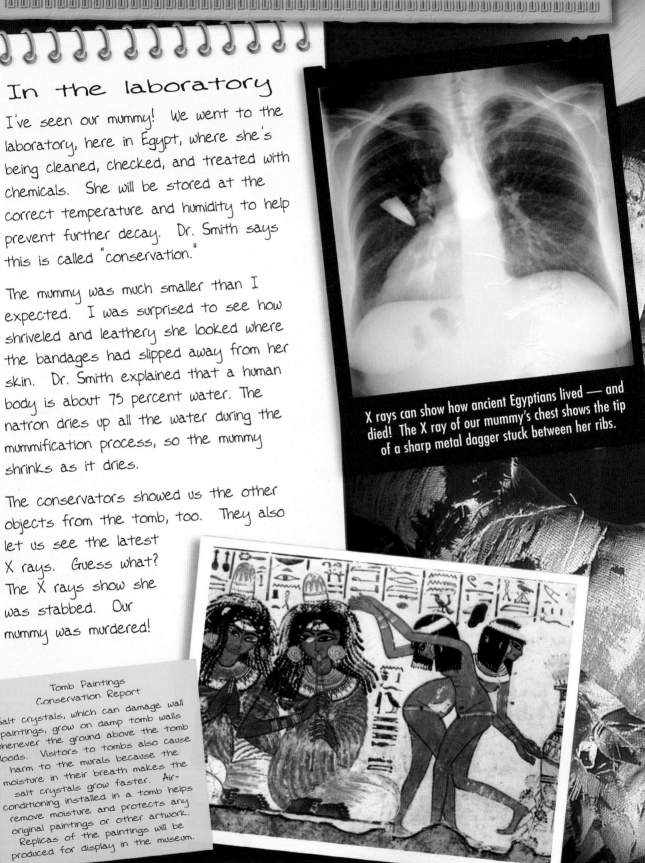

X rays can show how ancient Egyptians lived — and died! The X ray of our mummy's chest shows the tip of a sharp metal dagger stuck between her ribs.

Tomb Paintings Conservation Report

Salt crystals, which can damage wall paintings, grow on damp tomb walls whenever the ground above the tomb floods. Visitors to tombs also cause harm to the murals because the moisture in their breath makes the salt crystals grow faster. Air-conditioning installed in a tomb helps remove moisture and protects any original paintings or other artwork. Replicas of the paintings will be produced for display in the museum.

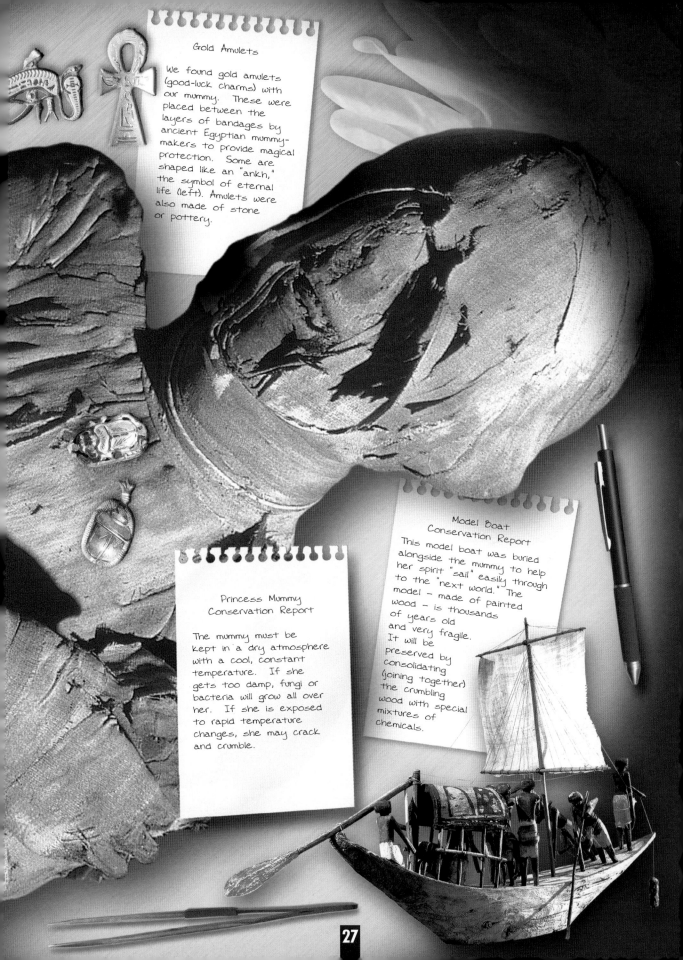

Gold Amulets

We found gold amulets (good-luck charms) with our mummy. These were placed between the layers of bandages by ancient Egyptian mummy-makers to provide magical protection. Some are shaped like an "ankh," the symbol of eternal life (left). Amulets were also made of stone or pottery.

Princess Mummy Conservation Report

The mummy must be kept in a dry atmosphere with a cool, constant temperature. If she gets too damp, fungi or bacteria will grow all over her. If she is exposed to rapid temperature changes, she may crack and crumble.

Model Boat Conservation Report

This model boat was buried alongside the mummy to help her spirit "sail" easily through to the "next world." The model — made of painted wood — is thousands of years old and very fragile. It will be preserved by consolidating (joining together) the crumbling wood with special mixtures of chemicals.

THE PRINCESS MUMMY

Famous at last

Wow! I'm going to be on TV. Our mummy is the subject of a documentary (a factual TV program), and the director wants all the museum team members to appear in it. We went to the studio today. I told the interviewer all about Great-Grandpa's travels, and Dr. Smith described our dig in Egypt.

Dr. Smith has been studying history books and poring over documents written by ancient Egyptian scribes trying to learn more about our mummy's life. The elaborate tomb and beautiful jewelry make Dr. Smith think that our mummy was a princess married to a pharaoh. According to murals in her tomb, she lived in a palace surrounded by beautiful gardens with musicians and dancers to entertain her. She probably ate good food like fresh fruits and vegetables, as well as meat from oxen, gazelles, and fish. But who killed her and why? Dr. Smith is writing a book to answer these questions. I can't wait to read it!

The mummy, her coffin, and a replica dagger are on display at the museum in Egypt. The TV camera crew set up its equipment to film the artifacts for the documentary.

THE PRINCESS MUMMY
The story of a murdered princess
Dr. Jane Smith and Dr. Mokhtar Ahmad

Shabti toys like these will be among the items sold in the City Museum's gift shop.

HISTORY TV

Script: The Princess Mummy

Camera shot 26 (Egypt, inside museum): Close-up of decorated golden coffin featuring the mummy's face.

Narrator: What tragic secrets hide behind this serene face? Why did such a young, beautiful woman die such a violent death? Dr. Jane Smith, Egyptologist at the City Museum, thinks she knows.

Camera shot 27 (studio): Cut to studio shot of Dr. Smith being interviewed.

Narrator: Dr. Smith, what's your theory about how this mummy died?

Dr. Smith: I think she was murdered by a jealous rival — probably after giving birth to a baby boy. Pharaohs had lots of wives. The wives who produced sons were favored over those who had only daughters or no children at all. Sometimes the wives who were angry about this treatment attacked the other royal wives who gave birth to sons.

Narrator: Thank you, Dr. Smith. That's an interesting theory.

Camera shot 28 (Egypt, inside museum): Fade out shot of mummy. Golden glow fills screen. Closing music begins softly, then volume slowly increases.

Camera shot 29: Fade into shot of sunset over the pyramids.

Narrator: Our beautiful mummy has kept her secret for over 3,500 years. Now, at long last, she can share it with us. Closing music, full volume.

Camera shot 30 (studio): Closing credits. Screen fades to black.

GLOSSARY

Ammut: a mythical, crocodile-headed creature that would eat the heart of the dead.

amulets: ancient Egyptian lucky charms.

Anubis: the jackal-headed ancient Egyptian god of the dead.

archaeologist: someone who studies the past by examining the artifacts left behind.

artifacts: objects made by humans, for example tools, pottery, jewelry, or statues.

bilharzia: a tropical disease passed to humans by snails. The snails release the eggs of parasitic worms called schistosomes into wetlands, rivers, or irrigation ponds. The eggs grow into larvae that burrow into the skin of humans and settle in the liver, kidneys, and intestines. They cause internal bleeding, inflammation, and organ enlargement. Infected humans also release eggs, which in turn can infect more snails. This disease is still very common in Egypt. It is also known as schistosomiais.

canopic jar: a vessel used to hold the internal organs of a mummified person.

conservation: the scientific process of cleaning, mending, and preserving something.

curator: senior museum staff member, usually in charge of its collections.

demotic (writing): a simplified type of hieroglyphic writing used for business and religious works.

Egyptologist: a person who studies all aspects of ancient Egyptian life.

excavation: the removal of the top layers to expose what's underneath.

Eye of Horus: a protective symbol of the falcon-headed god of light and the sky. *See also* wedjat.

faience: (fay-**ontz**) a blue-green material made from crushed quartz mixed with ash and lime that was used to make jewelry and to decorate pottery.

felucca: a boat with a shallow hull and large sails used by modern-day sailors on the Nile River.

fertile: capable of producing an abundance of crops or other products.

fiber optics: thin fibers of glass or plastic that carry light and images.

Giza: a city on the west bank of the Nile in northern Egypt that is home to the famous pyramids.

hieroglyphs: pictures used in Egyptian writing that represent words or groups of words.

hummus: a food made of garbanzo beans and oil.

jackal: a small, doglike African animal with large ears, long legs, and a bushy tail.

Karnak: a city just north of Luxor that is the site of many ancient temples and a sacred lake.

kiln: a special oven where pottery is baked at very high temperatures.

Lake Nasser: the lake created by the construction of the Aswan High Dam.

lapis lazuli: a rich, blue, semiprecious stone often used in jewelry, pottery, and wall murals.

linen: cloth woven from the strong, woody fibers of the flax plant.

malnutrition: a condition that results from a diet lacking the correct nutrients, vitamins, and minerals necessary for a healthy existence.

mummies: bodies wrapped in fabric that have been preserved through the mummification process.

mummification: the process of wrapping and preserving dead bodies.

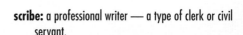

natron: moisture-absorbing salty crystals that were used to make mummies.

next world: according to the ancient Egyptians, a place where people's spirits went after death.

nilometer: a series of steps or a tall pillar marked in bands that were used to measure the level of Nile River flooding.

Nut: the ancient Egyptian goddess of the sky.

papyrus: a tall, reedlike plant used for making paper, boats, and sandals.

parasites: an animal that lives off an animal or a plant.

pathologist: a doctor who studies body tissues and fluids, including those of dead people, to discover how diseases cause change in a body.

pharaoh: a ruler of ancient Egypt.

pneumoconiosis: a lung disease caused by inhaling tiny particles of sand, dust, or powders; also called silicosis.

pyramid: a four-sided monument or building with sloping sides that meet at a point.

Rosetta stone: a black stone carved with figures in three languages — hieroglyphics, demotic writing, and Greek — that held the clues for understanding and translating the messages of the hieroglyphs.

silicosis: *See* pneumoconiosis.

scarab dung beetle: a stone, metal, or faience charm shaped like a beetle that was carried for good luck.

scribe: a professional writer — a type of clerk or civil servant.

shabti: a small magical figure buried with the dead to carry out work on behalf of the dead person in the next world.

Sphinx: an ancient Egyptian stone sculpture with a human head and the body of a lion.

stele: a stone or wooden pillar with carvings that tell a story or have religious significance.

Step Pyramid: Pharoah Zoser's pyramid at Giza, the very first pyramid ever built.

surveyor: a worker who measures land.

Thebes: the ancient capital of upper Egypt, now known as Luxor.

tomb: a grave, chamber, or vault for a dead body.

tunic: a plain garment with or without sleeves, usually worn belted at the waist.

Valley of the Kings: an area on the west bank of the Nile River across from Thebes in upper Egypt where many pharaohs were buried.

wedjat: an Egyptian symbol shaped like an eye that was considered a sign of protection and often used to decorate coffins. *See also* Eye of Horus.

MORE INFORMATION

BOOKS

Archaeology: The Study of Our Past. Investigating Science (series). (Gareth Stevens)

The Big Book of Mummies. Claire Llewellyn (NTC/Contemporary)

The Egyptian News. History News (series). Scott Steedman (Gareth Stevens)

Lift the Lid on Mummies: Unravel the Mysteries of Egyptian Tombs and Make Your Own Mummy! Jacqueline Dineen (Running Press)

Mummies and Their Mysteries. Charlotte Wilcox (Carolrhoda Books)

Mummies of the Pharaohs: Exploring the Valley of the Kings. Melvin Berger (National Geographic)

WEB SITES

www.guardians.net/egypt/kids/index.htm
Build your own pyramid!

www.neferchichi.com.html
Explore Neferchichi's tomb.

www.memphis.edu/egypt
Describes various archeological sites in Eypt.

www.pbs.org/wbgh/nova/pyramid/
Wander through the pyramids.

VIDEO

Mummies and Pyramids: Egypt and Beyond (series).

(World Almanac Video)

INDEX

Abu Simbel 7, 9
Ammut 11
amulets 27
ankh 27
antechamber 8–9
Anubis 11
archaeologist 8, 16, 17, 19, 22, 24, 28
Aswan High Dam 7, 9, 14, 15

bilharzia 25
burnishing 10

Cairo 6, 10, 14, 24
canopic jars 22
Carter, Howard 8, 9, 22
Champollion, Jean-Francois 19
coffins 8, 11, 22, 23, 24, 28, 29
cosmetics 20, 21, 23
CT scans 24
curator 4

dagger 28
demotic writing 19
documentary 28

Egyptologist 4, 21
endoscopes 24, 25
excavation 8, 9, 24

faience 10, 20
felucca 15
fiber optics 22

Giza 7, 12, 13, 14

Herodotus 22
hieroglyphics 18, 19
Horus, Eye of 25
hummus 6

jackal 11
jewelry 9, 20, 21, 23, 28

Karnak 7
kiln 10

Lake Nasser 9
lapis lazuli 21
linen 20, 22, 23

makeup 21, 23
mortuary 13, 18
mummies 8, 10, 11, 13, 22, 23, 24, 25, 26, 27, 28, 29
mummification 22
murals 11, 22, 26, 28

natron 20, 22, 26
next world 9, 10, 22, 23, 27
Nile River 6, 7, 8, 14, 15, 24
nilometer 15
Nut 11

oases 14

papyrus 14, 20, 23
parasites 25

perfume 21
pharaohs 1, 8, 12, 13, 19, 28, 29
pillars 18
pyramids 6, 12, 13, 29

robots 22
Rosetta stone 19

scarab dung beetle 5
scribes 19, 28
shabtis 4, 9, 10, 20, 23, 28
Sphinx 12, 13
spirits 9, 10, 11, 23, 27
stele 18, 19
stonemasons 12

temples 7, 9
tombs 4, 8, 9, 10, 18, 19, 20, 22, 26, 28

Valley of the Kings 7, 8

wedjat 25